GEOLOGY
OUR CHANGING EARTH

Sue Diffenderfer, Joey Tanner,
and Carolyn Zolg

Self-directed study units
for grades K–3 and 4–8.

Process- and product-oriented
interdisciplinary learning through:

Evaluating
Imagining
Researching
Reporting
Thinking and reacting
Mapping and charting
Creating and appreciating
Classifying and comparing
Career exploration and goal clarification

Zephyr Press
Tucson, Arizona

GEOLOGY
Our Changing Earth

Grades K-8

© 1983, 1993 by Zephyr Press.
Printed in the United States of America

ISBN 0-913705-04-7

Editor: Stacey Shropshire
Book Design and Production: Nancy Taylor

Zephyr Press
P.O. Box 13448
Tucson, Arizona 85732-3448

Contents

The Premise

Learning Is Natural

*Children are active participants in their
learning, not passive vessels to be filled.*

*They are always seeking and choosing what
they will learn and what they will not learn.*

*Their interest, trust, and active
involvement are crucial.*

*Children tend to become personally involved in
projects that appeal to a variety of modalities . . .
reading, writing, reasoning, building,
imagining, and creating.*

*What a gift we give when we respect the child's
natural need to explore, to reflect,
to communicate, to dream, to celebrate!*

(Available in poster form from Zephyr Press)

A Word to the Teacher

GEOLOGY

Geology is the story of this fluctuating ball of land and water told by geologists.

Earth's crust is like a mass of stiff taffy: it bulges, stretches, and is squeezed together by powerful forces within. If you were far out in space, watching Earth, and time were speeded up so that thousands of years would seem like a second, Earth would look like a living, pulsing globe.

Mountains would rise up, crumble, fold, and then be worn down flat. Seas would advance over the land and then drain away. Volcanoes would burst up through the ocean and form new islands. Other lands would sink slowly beneath the sea. The very continents would break apart, then fuse again in other places.

These forces are still at work all around us, slowly, slowly re-creating our world.

Rationale for Self-directed Learning

Our children's education must be more than the memorization of capitals of states, products of countries, and dates and places of past wars. Most teachers and parents would agree that what is also wanted is for our children to learn to think for themselves, to make wise choices, to work independently, to evaluate the results of their study thoughtfully, and to use their knowledge and skills creatively.

Obstacles to Independent Learning

In spite of the teacher's best efforts, many, if not most, classroom programs involve students in schedules and organizational plans that foster dependence rather than the independence we prefer. Students are told what is to be learned and how long it will take them to learn it. The teacher not only defines the resources but also decides whether the learning experience was a satisfactory and valuable one.

A Learning Atmosphere

Each time we, as educators, focus on what our objectives are, we need to take a fresh look at our classroom mode of operation and evaluate the effectiveness of the way we teach. Quite naturally, for most of us, our teaching style has had more to do with how we were taught than with what recent research has shown about the learning process. Even our good instincts have been overcome by the years of conditioning we have known in our own educational processes.

Like a breath of fresh air, recent findings from research on the brain support our intuitive knowledge. This research shows that our brains are receptive to learning only under certain conditions. Our job is to translate that information into a classroom atmosphere that provides

- challenge
- freedom within structure
- trust and warmth
- recognition of each student's learning process
- opportunities to experience success
- personal involvement in the curriculum

A natural transition generally occurs that transforms the former "teacher-lecturer" into a "fellow learner." As fellow learner, the teacher becomes a resource person, a facilitator, and a classroom manager. In this maturing atmosphere, students gradually come to see themselves as responsible for their own learning, and a foundation for self-direction is set.

At this point, an unexpected problem sometimes arises. We find students no more ready for their independent learning than we, as teachers, were ready to allow it. This common occurrence is mentioned repeatedly in the literature dealing with programming for the gifted, an area in which independent study and research are recommended as major curricular activities. See Suggested Readings.

From Passive Learner
to Active Participant

(Bridging the Gap)

The Zephyr self-directed study unit was developed expressly to bridge that gap: to transport the student from the position of passive recipient to that of an active participant in his/her own pursuit of knowledge.

Within the defined structure of each unit, students are given opportunities to

- make choices
- learn at their own paces
- learn in a manner suited to their own learning styles
- expand their research skills
- use a variety of modalities
- plan their own time
- develop the skills of creative, critical, and evaluative thinking
- experience whole-brain learning

Because assuming responsibility for directing their own learning is often an unfamiliar situation for students, they will need your encouragement at the start. Generally within six to nine weeks most students will be well on their way from teacher-dependence to self-motivation. (Beginning the venture with only à few choices, then gradually arranging the setting so that there are more and more choices works best.) As students assume more responsibility, many teachers begin to consider the school library as just another part of the classroom. The benefits are many, from gaining a personal relationship with the librarian to learning about the enormous resources available in most school libraries.

Eventually, a few students will be ready for a true investigative research study of professional quality as suggested by Joseph Renzulli in *Enrichment Triad Model: A Guide for Developing Defensible Programs for the Gifted and Talented*, 1977.

The Format

These units were originally developed for gifted students, but we now recognize that every child is gifted in one or more of the multiple intelligences. The units emphasize the use of higher-level thinking skills and are appropriate for use in any classroom where the goal is to encourage students to become responsible for their own education.

Interdisciplinary in content, each unit envelops a broad view of the topic by integrating the "basics" into each activity.

Within this book are two complete units: one created for the lower elementary student and one for the upper elementary student. Suggestions for adapting or adjusting either of the levels to fit any individual classroom are included.

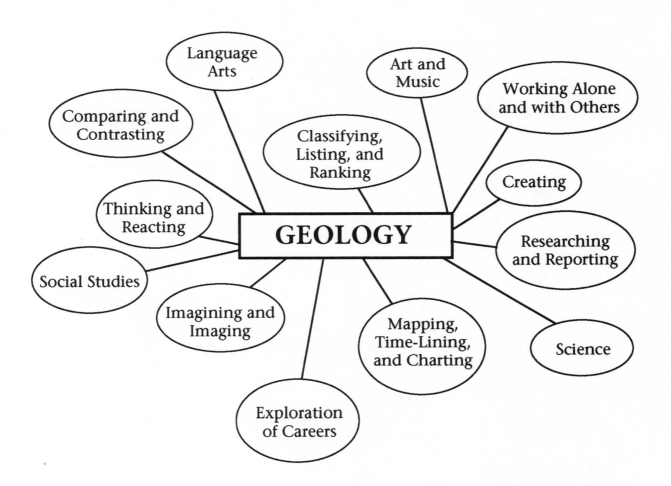

Suggested Readings

Self-directed Study

Armstrong, Thomas. *In Their Own Way: Discovering and Encouraging Your Child's Personal Learning Style.* Los Angeles: J. P. Tarcher, 1988.

Brewer, Chris, and Don G. Campbell. *Rhythms of Learning: Creative Tools for Developing Lifelong Skills.* Tucson, Ariz.: Zephyr Press, 1991.

Clark, Barbara. *Optimizing Learning.* Columbus, Ohio: Merrill Publishing Company, 1986.

Gallagher, James. *Teaching the Gifted Child.* 3d ed. Boston: Allyn & Bacon, 1985.

Gardner, Howard. *Frames of Mind: The Theory of Multiple Intelligences.* New York: Basic Books, 1985.

Kline, Peter. *The Everyday Genius: Restoring Children's Natural Joy of Learning.* Arlington, Va.: Great Ocean, 1988.

Maker, C. J. *Curriculum Development for the Gifted.* Rockville, Md.: Aspen Systems Corporation, 1982.

Malehorn, Hal. *Open to Change: Options for Teaching Self-directed Learners.* Palo Alto, Calif.: Scott Foresman and Company, 1978.

Miller, Ron. *What Are Schools For? Holistic Education in American Culture.* Brandon, Vt.: Holistic Education Press, 1990.

Purkey, William, and John Novak. *Inviting School Success: A Self-Concept Approach to Teaching and Learning.* 2d ed. Belmont, Calif.: Wadsworth Publishing Company, 1984.

Renzulli, Joseph. *Enrichment Triad Model: A Guide for Developing Defensible Programs for the Gifted and Talented.* Mansfield, Conn.: Creative Learning Press, 1977.

Stoddard, Lynn. *Redesigning Education: A Guide for Developing Human Greatness.* Tucson, Ariz.: Zephyr Press, 1991.

Udall, Anne J., and Joan E. Daniels. *Creating the Thoughtful Classroom: Strategies to Promote Student Thinking.* Tucson, Ariz.: Zephyr Press, 1991.

Getting Started

1. Select a topic as an extension of a regular subject (particularly when your class seems to crave more), or select a topic to pursue that is of particular interest and may not be a part of the curriculum. To zero in on special interests, administer an interest survey to each student.

2. Copy the unit for each student. When using these units for the entire class, you may want to expand or delete activities for individual students.

3. Set up a center in the classroom that encourages exploration in the subject field. You'll want to include a variety of materials. Be creative—the purpose of the center is to excite the students, so begin with lots of hands-on materials. Allow for ample browsing time and encourage students to investigate and become absorbed.

4. Go over each activity in the unit with the students, discussing and answering any questions. You, as teacher, are the key to successful implementation. Because most children are already well versed in the "One Right Answer" game, they will need encouragement to branch out into many of the open-ended activities in the packets.

5. Set the stage. Plan conferences and provide resources as needed. Then, get out of the way and let your students learn.

6. Give as much time as each student needs to complete each activity in the unit. The entire packet might take from five to ten weeks or longer.

7. As each activity is completed and evaluated, initial the activity near each number. You will want to evaluate on the basis of the response that is appropriate for each individual student.

8. When a student shows extreme interest in the topic, the completion of this unit might be only the beginning. This student may be ready for further study and research and may need only resources, guidance, and freedom to pursue his/her well-planned project.

Interest Development Center
GEOLOGY

The purpose of this interest center is to stimulate interest in the topic area. Students need time for browsing and investigating for maximum benefit. To expedite the exploration process, you might make the following materials available. These are beginning ideas; you and your students will think of more. Let parents and other teachers know about the center, and it will grow without effort.

BOOKS, VIDEOS, FILMSTRIPS, FILM LOOPS, POSTERS ABOUT

Earthquakes
Volcanoes
Rocks
Glaciers
Crystals
Jewels
Jewelry making
Coal
Caves and caving
Rock formations
Geologic ages
Oceanography
Tides
Undersea explorations
Pollution
Energy sources
Sonar
Rivers of the world
Aurora borealis
Plate tectonics

MAPS

A globe (relief, if possible)
A relief map of the world
Peters's map from UNICEF
Atlas of the world
Historical atlases
Old world and other world maps
Earth's features from space

ARTIFACTS

Fossils
Seashells
Microscope
Coal
Rocks
Jewels
Crystals
Rock tumbler

MUSIC

Recordings of waves, rain
and other weather

To Prepare for Further Research

Students will need to decide:

- What will the study be? What will be investigated and produced?

- Where will the background information be found (e.g., speaker, interviews, books, film, microfiche, documents)?

- What, exactly, will be the form of the product: a model, a manuscript, or . . . ?

- Who might be interested in the product: professionals in the field, publishers, organizations, or . . . ?

- What is needed to begin: specific plans, resources, deadlines, or . . . ?

Suggestions for Adapting the Unit to Your Particular Learning Situation

- Require fewer, or more, research sources.

- Assign more of the activities to small groups instead of to individual students.

- Give fewer or more choices.

- Delete some activities altogether.

- Arrange the unit as a class project with students choosing different parts to complete.

- Add some activities of your own.

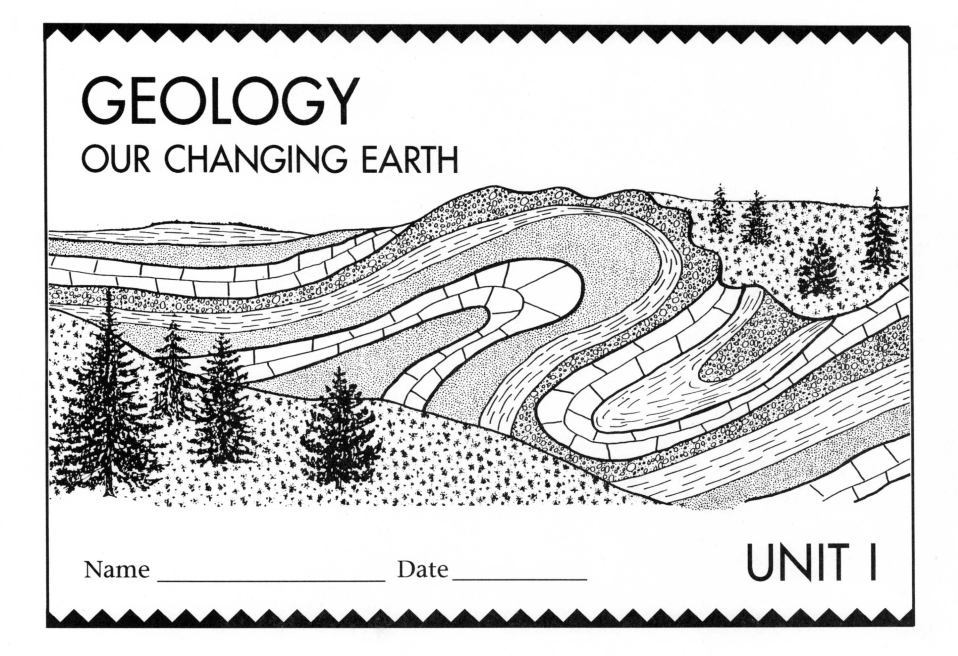

GEOLOGY
OUR CHANGING EARTH

Name _____ Date _____

UNIT I

1. EARTH TALK

Tsunami   Limestone
Speleology   Glaciers
Spelunking   Volcanoes
Sedimentary   Earthquake
Metamorphic   Delta
Igneous   Levee

● Create an illustrated picture book showing the meaning of each of these words.

2. EARTH'S BEGINNINGS

Our star, the sun, is one of 200 billion stars in the Milky Way galaxy. The universe contains at least 100 billion other galaxies.

Each of these contains at least 100 billion stars.

Think about planet Earth. Imagine that you are far out in space looking back at our great sphere. With your expert vision, see the land with its tall mountains, its green valleys, and its dry deserts. Notice the water—peaceful lakes, forceful rivers and oceans, salty seas, tropical rivers.

● Write down three descriptions of how Earth could have been formed. Be creative!

OR

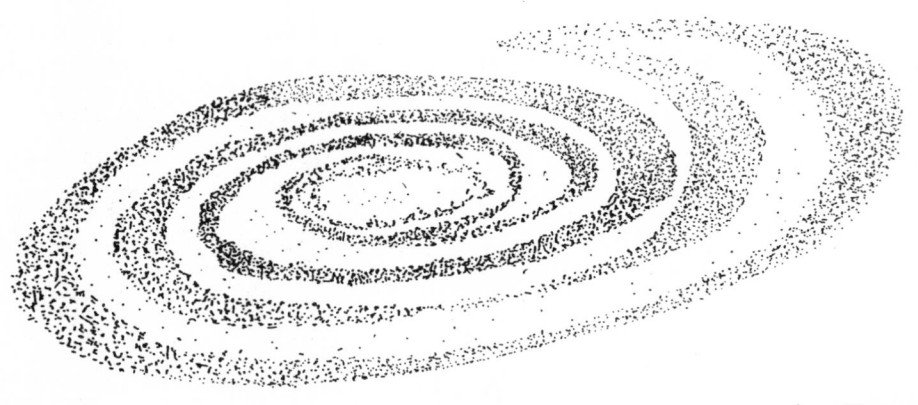

(continued on next page)

GEOLOGY Unit I © 1993 Zephyr Press, Tucson, AZ

2. EARTH'S BEGINNINGS (continued)

● Watch the "Rite of Spring" segment in Walt Disney's *Fantasia.* Make a list of the feelings you experience while you are watching—scared, hot, excited, bored, or . . . ? Write a poem using your words.

OR

● Write a description of how another planet, such as Mars or Saturn, could have been formed.

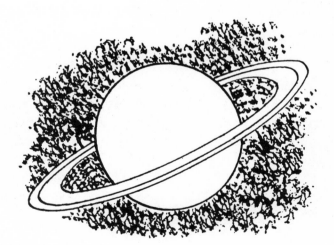

3. EARTH, THE PLANET

Earth is a rocky mass, 8,000 miles from surface to surface.

It is the third planet from the sun.

- Make a time line showing the geologic ages of Earth. Include some of the plants and animals that lived in each age.

  OR

- Create a mobile showing Earth, the sun, and the other planets. Be sure to put the planets in the right order, and to make the smallest planet the smallest in your mobile, the biggest the biggest.

  OR

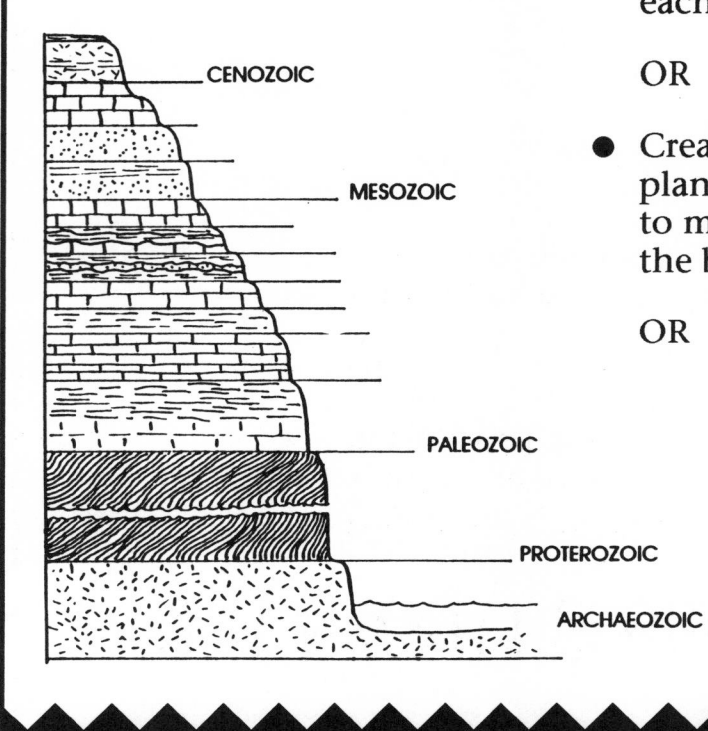

CENOZOIC

MESOZOIC

PALEOZOIC

PROTEROZOIC

ARCHAEOZOIC

(continued on next page)

3.   EARTH, THE PLANET (continued)

Find out what Pangaea is.

- Draw a picture of what you think it might have looked like. Include the animals and plants you think might have lived there.

   OR

Read *How to Dig a Hole to the Other Side of the Earth* by Faith McNulty.

- Act out each segment for your class. Really imagine how each stage would make you feel.

4. MAGNETIC POLES

Find out about the compass and how it is related to the North and South poles.

- Make your own compass. Teach at least one person how it works.

    OR

Find out about the people who discovered the North and South poles. Imagine you are one of them about to set out.

- Make a list of everything you will need on your expedition.

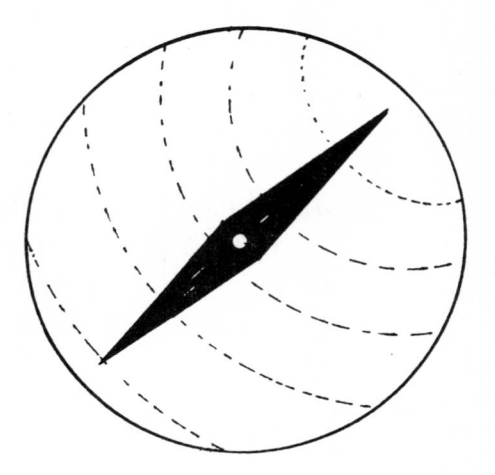

5. WATER OF EARTH

Water seems weak, but slowly over years and years, the waves break off pieces of the shore and the rain wears away mountains.

- List at least 20 adjectives describing water, then write a poem, a song, or a story using your words.

    OR

- Create a collage showing changes in Earth that resulted from water.

    OR

- Write a news flash about an impending disaster involving water.

    OR

- Make a chart showing the water cycle.

6. ROCK

CHOOSE ONE

- Create a slide show that illustrates how one kind of rock changes into another.

- Design a mobile showing the uses of coal.

- On a chart, classify rocks in as many ways as possible.

- Prepare a 10-card fact file on your favorite jewels.

- Create a filmstrip showing the life cycle of a piece of chalk.

- Put together a booklet illustrating equipment used by a miner.

(continued on next page)

6. ROCK (continued)

Find out about the different kinds of mines and then find out if there is or ever was any mining around where you live.

- Create a collection of rocks that were mined in your area.

Find out what minerals are valuable today that weren't valuable in the past, or what are not valuable today that were in the past.

- Create a poster with a time line showing what happened to make these minerals more valuable or less valuable.

7. CHANGING EARTH

If you were out in space and time was speeding up, Earth would look like a living, pulsing globe.

Choose one of these powerful forces of change:

> Glaciers
> Volcanoes
> Earthquakes

Find out everything you can about it.

- Then report your findings to your class in a

    filmstrip
    slide show
    chart
    model
    tape recording or
    your choice

    OR

(continued on next page)

7. CHANGING EARTH (continued)

Find out about different kinds of weather: hurricanes, tornadoes, monsoons, windstorms, or any others you might think of. What causes them? What do they cause?

- ● Make a diagram showing the causes of each and present it to the class.

8. SAVING EARTH'S RESOURCES

RESEARCH

Water pollution
Sources of fresh water
New construction in your community
Rain forest destruction
Natural habitats of endangered species

● Select one of these and tell your class about it.

OR

Find out what an ecosystem is. Decide which ecosystem you live in, and find out what humans are doing that hurts the plants and animals in your ecosystem.

● Explain to your class what humans could do instead that does not hurt your ecosystem.

9. SPELEOLOGY

Imagine that you are an experienced caver.

You have been on assignment to explore a cave and present your findings to *National Geographic*.

- Create a presentation with maps, charts, slides, filmstrips, and anything else you think would be helpful to help people understand your cave better. Give your presentation to the class, if you would like.

  OR

- Write a play about five people who are the first ones to find and explore a cave.

10. YOUR COMMUNITY
(City and State)

Explore the natural area where you live. Look for

      Examples of different kinds of rocks
      Evidence of plate tectonics, volcanoes, and earthquakes
      Information about the water supply
      Natural deposits in the ground such as clay, soda, lime, coal, oil
      Fossils

Look through travel guides and/or interview an experienced speleologist.

● Prepare a booklet for your
   library or historical society.

   OR

(continued on next page)

10. YOUR COMMUNITY
(City and State) (continued)

Go to a cemetery near your home and look at the different headstones and the dates on them.

- Write a report explaining why those with older dates have more rounded edges and less clear lettering than those with newer dates.

  OR

Go to a library, museum, or another building that has a marble floor. Look carefully in the floor for evidence of fossils.

- Create a photo portfolio of the fossils you find. Take your best guess at identifying each one.

GEOLOGY
OUR CHANGING WORLD

Name _____ Date _____

UNIT II

1. EARTH TALK

Marianas Trench	Paleontology
Plate tectonics	Sedimentary
Core sampler	Metamorphic
San Andreas Fault	Igneous
Richter scale	Limestone
Tsunami	Great Ice Age
Ring of fire	Mantle
Continental shelf	Delta
Spelunking	Levee
Vesuvius	Atoll
Biosphere	Trilobite
Geothermal	Archaeology

Look up these words and understand them before you begin your study.

Choose three of the words.

- Create a photo portfolio that illustrates your three words.

2. EARTH'S BEGINNINGS

Research different theories of how Earth was formed. How have these theories changed over the centuries?

- Create a poster of a time line of the different theories. Be sure to explain why each one gave way to the next.

  OR

Find out about the contributions each of the following made to our understanding of Earth's geology.

Galileo   William Smith
Sir Isaac Newton   Charles Lyell
Ernest Rutherford   Louis Agassiz
James Hutton   Robert Mallet
James Hall   Van Allen

Choose three of these people.

- Draw a picture of what we would think Earth looked like if we didn't know what these people discovered.

3. EARTH, THE PLANET

Earth is primarily rock, 8,000 miles from surface to surface. Two-thirds of Earth is covered with water. It is the third planet from the sun.

Compare Earth's makeup to that of other planets in our solar system. What are the differences between the geology of planets closest to the sun and those farthest from the sun? How may these other planets have formed?

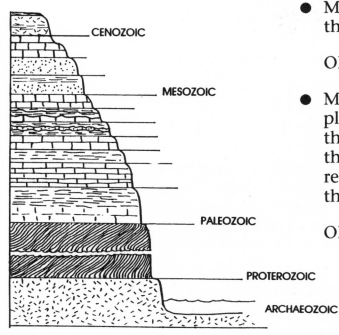

CENOZOIC

MESOZOIC

PALEOZOIC

PROTEROZOIC

ARCHAEOZOIC

● Make a filmstrip or an illustrated description of how these planets may have been formed.

OR

● Make accurate models of our sun, Earth, and two other planets in our solar system. Choose one that is closer to the sun than Earth, and one that is farther from the sun than Earth. Be sure to make the planets the right size in relation to the sun, and try to find a way to illustrate their different compositions, including their atmospheres.

OR

(continued on next page)

GEOLOGY Unit II © 1993 Zephyr Press, Tucson, AZ

3. EARTH, THE PLANET (continued)

Find out what is meant by "geological time."

● Write a report in which you set a scale of time we can understand equal to geological time. For instance, each century equals one day. Include the length of different eras, periods, and epochs, and the different animal and plant life that existed. For example, how many days ago did dinosaurs roam Earth?

OR

● Using a box of soft sand and different sized rocks, create craters by dropping the rocks into the sand. Experiment with different sizes of rocks and different heights from which you drop the rocks. Do the experiment in front of your class and explain the different types of craters that are formed. Compare them to craters on an atlas of the moon.

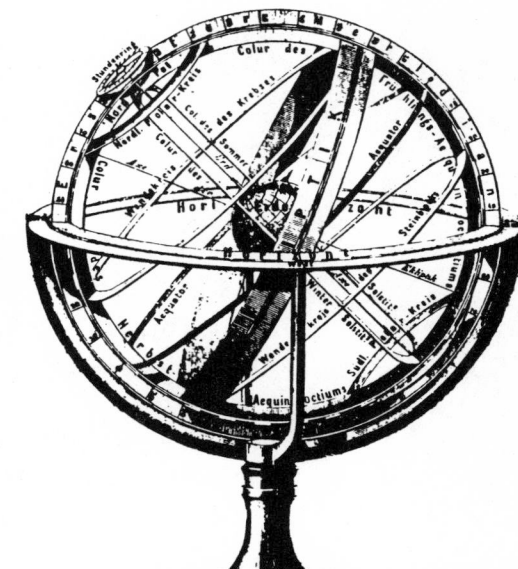

4. MAGNETIC POLES

Earth is like a giant magnet. Though its force is weak for its size, it works in the same way as a small magnet. It, too, has fields surrounding it in space. How are they related to Earth's rotation?

What are the magnetic poles? How are they different from the geographic poles? What do scientists mean when they say that the magnetic poles have wandered over the years, and how do they explain the phenomenon? Do we have a "wobbly" Earth?

Over each pole, colored light glows and shimmers high in the atmosphere.

Research the aurora borealis.

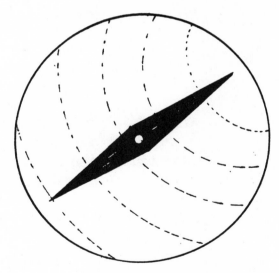

- Make a poster that shows what causes it.

  OR

(continued on next page)

4. MAGNETIC POLES (continued)

Read all you can about Earth and its center. Then be the first scientist to take a journey to the center of Earth.

- Keep a journal of each day's events on your way. Note the changes in each level you pass through.

    OR

Discover how gravity and tides are related. Read *World beneath the Waves* by Walter Buehr.

- With a friend, develop an experiment that will share your findings with your class.

5. WATER OF EARTH

We call our planet "Earth," but it might be more fitting to call it "water." Look at a globe and see if you agree with this statement.

Imagine a raindrop, snowflake, or hailstone tossed and blown in a storm, finally coming to rest on a hillside.

- Write a story depicting its many adventures. Take it eventually back to where it began. Will your story have an end?

OR

(continued on next page)

GEOLOGY Unit II © 1993 Zephyr Press, Tucson, AZ

5. WATER OF EARTH (continued)

Find out about different kinds of bodies of water: artesian wells, lakes, rivers, streams, oceans, seas, and bays are just a few. Choose one type that is near you or imagine that you have one near you. (If you are imagining your body of water, give it a name.) Imagine that you are a resort representative trying to get people to come to your body of water. What can people do in your body of water that would make them want to come visit it for a vacation?

● Create a brochure that tells people about your body of water.

OR

Research your favorite fish and find out if it needs fresh water, salt water, or brackish water to survive. Find out about fish or animals that live in each.

● Make a model of an animal or a fish from each kind of water. Include the adaptations that make it possible for the animal to live there.

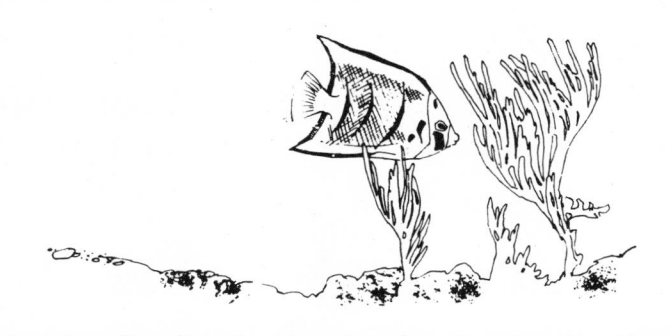

6. OCEANS

Find out how tides are caused. Where are the highest tides found? What shore animals use the tides' action to surface?

- Organize a display with books, posters, and filmstrips. Include any artifacts related to tides and any information you have compiled.

  OR

Find out about as many reports of sightings of sea serpents as possible. Include both ancient and modern reports. Is there sea serpent research going on today?

- List the similarities and differences among the different serpents.

  OR

- Create a news release warning fishers, the Navy, or coastline residents about ocean currents. First find out about

    the paths of the currents
    whether they are warm or cold
    how climate affects currents
    how currents are tracked and measured

  OR

(continued on next page)

6. OCEANS (continued)

Investigate the seven seas of ancient times. How many oceans do we count now?

- Create a chart contrasting the knowledge of oceans now and then.

  OR

- Write an editorial describing a solution to the problem of pollution developing in the oceans of the world. Which countries are the worst offenders? How might they change their practices?

7. THE OCEAN FLOOR

Research the ocean depths. Discover the underwater mountains, canyons, trenches, volcanoes, and creatures that live there.

- Create a papier-mâché model of the Atlantic or Pacific seascapes. Include islands, continental shelves, slopes, and the mid-ocean trenches. Paint your model, making different depths different colors.

  OR

- Assemble a display showing undersea explorations, sonar, possibilities for living under the sea, a core sampler, or some other aspect of the undersea world that interests you.

8. LAKES

As beautiful and permanent as our lakes may seem, they are short-lived by geologic standards and are hardly more than puddles on our planet.

- Create a poster showing a simple drawing of at least six different types of lakes. List the attributes of each one.

  OR

- Make a filmstrip or slide show showing the step-by-step formation of the Great Lakes. Include your hypothesis regarding their future.

9. RIVERS

Find out about the controversy regarding the building of the Glen Canyon Dam on the Colorado River.

- Organize and present a debate on whether the dam should have been built.

  OR

- Build a papier-mâché model of at least three of the world's mightiest rivers. Prepare a poster or pamphlet that tells the story of the rivers' origins, their changes, how life is affected along their banks, and how people use the rivers. Are the rivers considered "wild" or "tamed"?

  OR

GEOLOGY Unit II © 1993 Zephyr Press, Tucson, AZ

9. RIVERS (continued)

The excitement of following a river that people don't know a lot about has captured many an adventurous heart. Read about some of the following explorers, or find your own real-life or fictional explorer to read about.

John Wesley Powell

Mary Kingsley

Lewis and Clark and Sacagawea

David Livingstone

Huckleberry Finn

● Report about your explorer to your class.

OR

GEOLOGY Unit II © 1993 Zephyr Press, Tucson, AZ

9. RIVERS (continued)

Find out about water rights and water ownership in the United States.

- Write a proposal that gives possible solutions to the following problem. Be sure to consider both people's rights and make sure your solutions don't favor one person over the other. Both people should get the water they need.

One person buys land along a river and uses the water for his fields. Years later, another person builds a home upstream and drains off much of the water, so the river is dry where the first person lives.

Page 3

10. GROUNDWATER

The surface of Earth is soaked with water. It seeps down and down through all the cracks and tiny spaces of the soil, collecting into what is called the "water table." The water table may be above ground or below ground. Where does it go from there? What makes the level change?

- Chart the water table of your community from 1900 to the present. What alternative sources of fresh water are there?

    OR

Contact your local water company or city water department. Find out where your community gets its water. Find out if there is a pollution problem or a potential pollution problem, or a water shortage.

- Design a brochure urging people to take action. Distribute it.

    OR

(continued on next page)

10. GROUNDWATER (continued)

Choose a Native American tribe that lived in your area before it was settled by other Americans. Find out how they viewed water and how they used it and conserved it.

- Write a play depicting the benefits or drawbacks of their attitudes toward water.

  OR

- Keep a journal of all the times your family uses water for one week. Choose three to five practices that waste water, and make a chart showing how much water would be saved if your family would do something else.

11. ROCKS

In the Hindu religion there is a goddess, Kali, who represents the force of creation and destruction. How can something be both creative and destructive at the same time? Think about this as you learn about the life cycle of rocks.

Research the three basic forms of rocks and how one turns into another. When does a rock reach the end of its changing?

- Make a filmstrip or slide show to illustrate these changes.

  OR

Read *The Curious World of Crystals* by Lenore Sanders, or another book about crystals. Research natural crystals and learn to identify at least three.

- Make crystal candy or a crystal garden. Experiment by letting some of your solutions cool at room temperature and putting similar solutions in the refrigerator or freezer to cool faster. Observe your creations under a microscope.

  OR

GEOLOGY Unit II © 1993 Zephyr Press, Tucson, AZ

11. ROCKS (continued)

- Make a 20-card fact file about gold, silver, and copper. Include why they are valuable, how they combine with other minerals and elements, and how people use each one.

    OR

Find out how different minerals are used in industry.

- Choose one rock and demonstrate to your class, on a small scale, how it is used in industry.

    OR

Remember the last time you went to the blackboard. Think about the piece of chalk you held in your hand. Packed into that cylinder are the remains of billions of tiny one-celled sea animals. Imagine the journey of chalk from sea bottom to cliffs to factory.

- Write a story or poem called "The Early Life of a Piece of Chalk."

    OR

GEOLOGY Unit II © 1993 Zephyr Press, Tucson, AZ

11. ROCKS (continued)

Find out about the two different kinds of meteorites. How was each type formed? Why are they different?

- Find some examples of each type of meteorite and give a presentation to the class in which you tell what you know.

  OR

- Show how fossils are created by making an impression in the sand and then making a mold casting.

  OR

Find out what "fossil fuels" are. Compare them to other types of energy.

- Make a chart that depicts the types of energy there are, and include fossil fuels. Include the cost of each kind of fuel, how much of it there is, and how much or little it would pollute our air, water, or other natural resources.

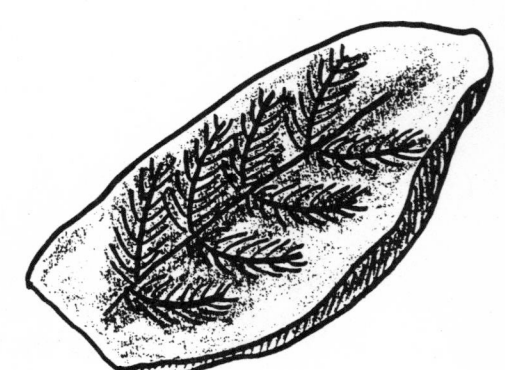

GEOLOGY Unit II © 1993 Zephyr Press, Tucson, AZ

12. CAVES

How many different types of caves are there? Research a few of them.

- Build a papier-mâché model of at least two types of caves.

  OR

- Create a mobile or chart showing the equipment used by a spelunker. If possible, invite a spelunker to speak to your class.

  OR

(continued on next page)

12. CAVES (continued)

You can remember the difference between stalactites and stalagmites in one of the following ways:

A stala**ctite** must hang **tight** to the ceiling or it will fall.

A stala**gmite** stands **might**ily up from the ground.

Stala**c**tite has a "c" in the word and hangs from the **c**eiling.

Stala**g**mite has a "g" in the word and stands on the **g**round.

● Draw a cross-sectional diagram of a limestone cave showing stalactites and stalagmites.

13. SALT

Trace the origins of these sayings:

"Back to the salt mines."

"Put salt on the bird's tail."

"Not worth his salt."

"Pouring salt in an open wound."

What do they mean today?

Research some of the sacred and superstitious beliefs related to salt.

- Create a book showing what you have learned.

  OR

Investigate floating in a swimming pool versus floating in the ocean.

- Write a report or tell your class why people float and how salt influences floating.

14. CHANGING EARTH

Choose two of the following.

Find out what Pangaea is. Imagine what Earth looked like when Pangaea existed.

- Draw a map of the different countries that might exist. Color the different climate zones different colors and create a legend for your map.

  OR

Imagine that you are running for president of Pangaea.

- Create an election campaign that addresses particular problems Pangaeans might face.

  OR

GEOLOGY Unit II © 1993 Zephyr Press, Tucson, AZ

14. CHANGING EARTH (continued)

Find a map of ancient Earth. Mark where your town would be on that map. Is it under water?

- Draw a picture of what your town would look like if it were under water today.

    OR

Find out about the different forces that change our Earth. Focus on two that you think changed your part of Earth.

- Prepare a lesson plan and teach your class what happened.

    OR

Read *Islands of the Ocean* by Delia Goetz.

- Develop a "Who Am I?" quiz and give it to at least ten friends to find out how much they know about islands of the world and their origins. Record your results.

    OR

GEOLOGY Unit II © 1993 Zephyr Press, Tucson, AZ

14. CHANGING EARTH (continued)

Find out what humans are doing to change Earth. Are we doing anything that is changing Earth faster than it would normally change? Look specifically at our atmosphere, rain forests and other habitats, nuclear testing, etc.

- Write a scholarly report about these effects and what they may mean for us in the future.

  OR

Find out what is meant by the expression, "The present is the key to the past." Research a current change, such as a volcano, tsunami, hurricane, or something else, that has changed the world recently.

- Write a news report for a magazine about one of these changes.

GEOLOGY Unit II © 1993 Zephyr Press, Tucson, AZ

15. MAPS OF THE WORLD

Find out what "cartography" means. Research the history of cartography. How did people make maps before our present technology?

● Using one of the techniques we no longer use, make an accurate map of your neighborhood or your school. Include a legend of what different symbols mean, and decide how much distance one inch will stand for.

16. PLATE TECTONICS

Research the theory of plate tectonics.

Find a map that shows the outlines of the plates.

- Copy the map. Draw the outlines of the continents on the plates. Mark the areas where there are earthquakes, volcanoes, and mountain ranges. Notice which edges are crowding closer together and which are separating. Now cut the pieces apart. Notice areas that have "fused" together.

    OR

- Prepare and present a lesson to your class about plate tectonics. Discuss:

    How scientists measure the amount of drift.

    What is happening along the great Mid-Atlantic Rift.

    What may eventually happen to western California.

17. GLACIERS

Even now, huge masses of packed ice cover 10 percent of our planet, always slowly moving, carving, and shaping the land, carrying boulders thousands of miles, digging deep pits, scratching and scarring the land.

- Write and illustrate a book about glaciers for someone younger than you. Include the following information:

    How many ice ages have there been?

    What and when was the Great Ice Age?

    How much of Earth was covered?

    What happens when a glacier meets the ocean? A cliff?

    How can ice "bend"?

    What color is it inside a glacier?

    If Earth's climate warms up, will the ice caps grow or shrink?

    What are the differences between ice sheets and glaciers?

    OR

(continued on next page)

17. GLACIERS (continued)

- Draw a map of Earth as it would be if all the remaining glaciers rapidly melted.

  OR

There are boulders on the eastern coast of Britain made of a particular rock that is found only in Norway. Think like a scientist and hypothesize how they might have gotten there. Think of more than one theory and then make a case for your favorite.

- Present your ideas in a scholarly report. Cite your references.

GEOLOGY Unit II © 1993 Zephyr Press, Tucson, AZ

18. EARTHQUAKES

- Prepare at least ten questions and interview one or more people who have experienced an earthquake.

  OR

- Create a mobile of the most destructive tsunamis. Label it with the name, date, and distance each one traveled.

  OR

- Draw a map of the world and indicate the major earthquake areas.

  OR

(continued on next page)

18. EARTHQUAKES (continued)

Find out how earthquakes are predicted.

- Draw the San Andreas Fault and locate the earthquakes that have happened along its edges during the last 150 years. Circle the major quakes. Is there any pattern evident? Predict when you think another quake will come.

  OR

Learn how a seismograph works.

- Draw a diagram of a seismograph. Are there seismographs set up in your community? Arrange to visit one or have someone come to speak to your class about how they work.

19. VOLCANOES

Red-hot lava spilling down the sides of a volcano is obviously destructive. What are the other destructive forces? Imagine you have x-ray vision and can see what is happening as a volcano begins to build up.

- Make a drawing that shows the inside of the volcano. Attach some information about what you have learned. Include information about the source of the heat.

- Create a chart showing at least eight well-known volcanoes. Classify them according to type. Note the date of eruption, the country where they are found, and the amount of destruction.

- Make a filmstrip or slide show of how an undersea volcano can create an island and how the island then becomes a place of life.

20. EXPLORE YOUR COMMUNITY

Contact your local Federal Geological Office for help in learning about the geology of the land near your home. Then explore your community for unique and unusual geologic features. Look for rock formations, meteor craters, caves, old volcanoes, fossil beds. Imagine you are the first scientist to see the area. Visit it with a tape recorder, a pair of binoculars, and a magnifying glass. Try to find examples of igneous, sedimentary, and metamorphic rocks.

- Make notes describing your observations and reactions as you experience them.

   OR

Locate old photographs or descriptions of your community. Go back as far as you can. Compare then and now. How have people changed the natural landscape?

- List all the changes you can think of. Next to each change, write all the effects of the changes that you can imagine.

21. CAREERS

Choose two or three of the following career areas:

Geochemistry
Geophysics
Seismology
Oceanography
Paleontology
Soil conservation
Mining
Forest service
National Park Service
Energy conservation
Surveying

● Write for information about educational requirements and job opportunities to:

American Geological Institute
1444 N. Street, NW
Washington, D.C. 20005

● List six qualities necessary for each of the career areas you choose.

EXPLORING THE ARTS

*An opportunity to integrate art experiences
within an academic content area*

By Stephany Mack

While each component—the self-directed learning units and Exploring the Arts—
is a complete and valid learning experience in itself, together they provide a more
comprehensive and lasting educational experience for the learner.

MOTHER NATURE'S COLOR WHEEL

INVESTIGATE the area where you live. What are the colors of the earth? Is the ground a rich brown, black, grey, or red? Are the trees a deep dark green, yellow green, blue green, light green . . . ? What about mountains, hills, cliffs . . . ?

DESIGN A COLOR CHART

This BASIC COLOR VOCABULARY list will help you make your chart:

> HUE - the name of a color
> INTENSITY - the brightness of a color
> VALUE - the lightness and darkness of a color
> WARM COLORS - the sun colors . . . yellows, reds, oranges
> COOL COLORS - the water colors . . . blues, purples, greens

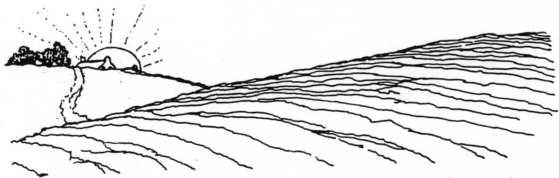

(continued on next page)

COLOR WHEEL (continued)

NOW . . .

LIST the geological characteristics of your landscape on the chart.

LIST the colors you observe.

DESCRIBE the intensities and values of the colors.

DIVIDE your geological characteristics into warm and cool color categories.

DRAW a picture of the landscape where you live. Use oil pastels or crayons to color it. Take your time to mix and blend colors.

REFER to your chart. Are you using all the colors in your landscape?

INVITE AN ARTIST

INVITE a goldsmith or silversmith to your classroom.

HINT: Check your telephone book under jewelers or artists. Or contact your local university or college art department for help in locating an artist.

ASK the artist to:

    demonstrate his/her craft.

    show slides and/or picture of his/her work.

    talk about the metals and jewels he/she uses.

DESIGNS BY MOTHER NATURE

THERE ARE MANY BEAUTIFUL DESIGNS IN NATURE

LOOK: at the cracks in mud dried by the sun
            at the veins in a leaf
            at the arrangement of flower petals
            at the ribs on a seashell
            at the movement of water

SELECT a design by Mother Nature. Use her art work as an inspiration for a design of your own.

HINT: use the same shapes and repeat them
           vary the sizes
           overlap the shapes
           change the direction of the shapes
           use paper at least 9" x 12" so you have room to
              experiment different ways

DRAW your design with ONE color marker. After you have completed the drawing, add color to it if you wish.

GEOLOGY Arts © 1993 Zephyr Press, Tucson, AZ

TEXTURES FROM NATURE

A RUBBING is a mark made by putting a soft piece of paper over an object and rubbing it with a crayon or pencil until the image "shows through" on the paper.

CREATE a design by taking rubbings from as many NATURAL objects as you can.

SOME IDEAS: the ground
                  seashells
                  tree bark
                  leaves and plants
                  rocks
                  fossils

Turn your paper at different angles so you rubbings will overlap. Use different colors for variety. Fill the paper with the rubbings.

HINT: Newsprint is an excellent weight paper to use.

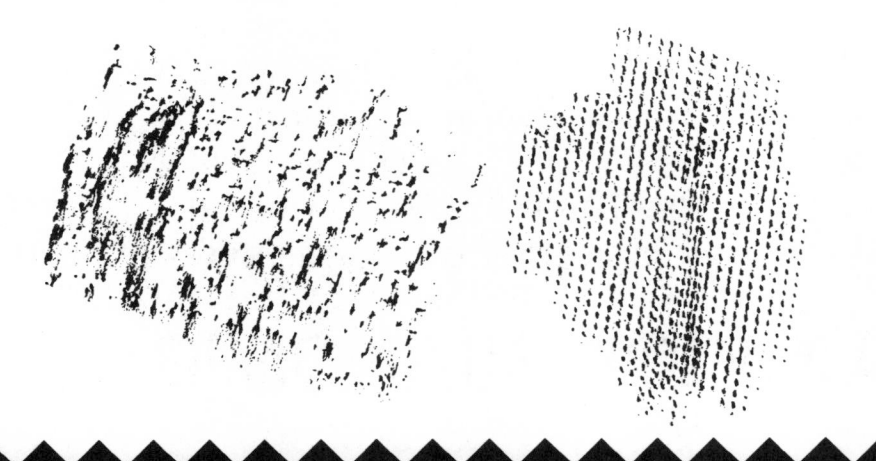

COMPARE & CONTRAST LANDSCAPE ARTISTS

Years ago a Dutch artist, **VINCENT VAN GOGH** (1853–1890), was painting landscapes. He is well known for his unique style of painting. His paintings are known for their movement; force; vigorous brush strokes; rough, textural surface quality; deep, rich color; expressive qualities.

COLLECT some art books with pictures of Vincent van Gogh's paintings.
STUDY his style of painting.
DISCUSS his stylistic characteristics with your classmates.

THEN . . .

INVESTIGATE the well-known American artist, **GEORGIA O'KEEFFE** (1887–1986). O'Keeffe moved to Santa Fe, New Mexico, from New York City to paint the desert. Her passion for the desert is reflected in her work. O'Keeffe's paintings are known for their rich pastel color; blended brush strokes; vast space; smooth textural, surface; quiet, still quality.

COLLECT some art books with pictures of Georgia O'Keeffe's paintings.
STUDY her style of painting.
DISCUSS her stylistic characteristics with your classmates.

WHEN YOU UNDERSTAND THE DIFFERENCES BETWEEN THE TWO ARTISTIC STYLES . . .

CHOOSE one style.
PAINT a landscape of your own.
HINT: Work on paper at least 18" x 24".

Expect to spend several hours on your painting as you develop the style in which you choose to work.

Bibliography

Baylor, Byrd. *Everybody Needs a Rock.* New York: Scribner's, 1974

Berger, Melvin. *As Old As the Hills.* New York: Franklin Watts, 1989.

Bramwell, Martyn. *Planet Earth.* New York: Franklin Watts, 1987.

Calder, Nigel. *The Restless Earth: A Report on the New Geology.* New York: Penguin, 1972.

Catherall, Ed. *Exploring Soil and Rocks.* Austin, Tex.: Stech-Vaughn, 1990.

Challand, Helen. *Activities in the Earth Sciences.* Chicago: Children's Press, 1982.

Cloud, Preston. *Oasis in Space.* New York: Norton, 1988.

Cole, Joanna. *The Magic School Bus: Inside the Earth.* New York: Scholastic, 1987.

Dixon, Dougal. *The Planet Earth.* New York: Macmillan, Aladdin, 1989.

Gang, Philip S. *Our Planet, Our Home: A Global Vision of Ecology.* Tucson, Ariz.: Zephyr, 1992.

Goldreich, Gloria, and Esther Goldreich. *What Can She Be: A Geologist.* New York: Lothrop, Lee and Shephard, 1976.

Keller, Peter. *Gemstones and Their Origins.* New York: Van Nostrand Reinhold, 1990.

Lambert, David. *The Field Guide to Geology.* New York: Facts on File, 1988.

Lauber, Patricia. *Volcano: The Eruption and Healing of Mount St. Helens.* New York: Bradbury, 1986.

Liptak/Steer. *Pangaea: The Mother Continent.* Tucson, Ariz.: Harbinger House, 1989.

Lye, Keith. *The Earth.* Morristown, N.J.: Silver Burdett, 1983.

Lye, Keith. *Rocks, Minerals, and Fossils.* Englewood Cliffs, N.J.: Silver Burdett, 1988.

McConnell, Anita. *The World Beneath Us*. New York: Facts on File, 1985.

McNulty, Faith. *How to Dig a Hole to the Other Side of the World*. New York: Harper and Row, 1979.

Marshall Cavendish Foundation. *The Earth*. New York: Marshall Cavendish Foundation, 1989.

Parker, Steve. *The Marshall Cavendish Science Project Book of the Earth*. New York: Marshall Cavendish Foundation, 1986.

Poth, Cathy. *The Earth*. New York: Silver Burdett Press, 1989.

Pough, Frederick. *Peterson's First Guide to Rocks and Minerals*. Boston: Houghton Mifflin, 1991.

Smith, P. J., ed. *The Earth*. New York: Macmillan, 1986.

Watson, Lyall. *The Water Planet*. Southbridge, Mass.: Crowne, 1988.

Zephyr Learning Packets—Self-Directed Study at Its Best!

Here are 26 jam-packed activity units that promote critical and creative thinking and provide students with hands-on problem-solving, research, and higher-level thinking skills. Students discover the excitement of self-directed study with these absorbing topics. The best part . . . you facilitate the process—your students do the learning.

The Learning Packets—
- **Are reproducible for each student**
- **Require student research and reporting**
- **Promote critical and creative thinking**
- **Need little teacher preparation or supervision**
- **Are easy to use**

Each Packet includes—
- **Interdisciplinary and integrative activities**
- **Complete bibliography**
- **Art exploration section**
- **Learning center ideas**
- **Two units: K–3 & 4–8**

Science Series

ROCKS AND MINERALS: Earth's Natural Wonders
by Carol Hauswald (1992)   ZP21-W . . . $19.95

FUTURISTICS: A Time to Come
by Joey Tanner (rev. 1992)   ZP03-W . . . $19.95

ARCHAEOLOGY
by Joey Tanner (1981)   ZP09-W . . . $19.95

MARINE BIOLOGY: The Ecology of the Sea
by Joey Tanner (rev. 1992)   ZP14-W . . . $19.95

GEOLOGY: Our Changing Earth
by Diffenderfer, Zolg, Tanner (1983)   ZP13-W . . . $19.95

PALEONTOLGY
by Joey Tanner (rev. 1992)   ZP15-W . . . $19.95

SCIENCE FICTION:
by Patricia Payson (1980)   ZM04-W . . . $19.95

ASTRONOMY
by Carolyn Zolg (rev. 1992)   ZP10-W . . . $19.95

ECOLOGY: Learning to Love Our Planet
by Susan Diffenderfer (1984)   ZP12-W . . . $19.95

ENTOMOLOGY
by Clements, Domin, Tanner (1983)   ZP12-W . . . $19.95

VOLCANOLOGY
by Bonnie Rasmussen (1983)   ZP16-W . . . $19.95

To order, write or call—

ZEPHYR PRESS
P.O. Box 13448-W
Tucson, Arizona 85732-3448
(602) 322-5090

Humanities and Social Studies Series

AMERICAN HISTORY
by Gael Beaham (rev. 1992)   ZM01-W . . . $19.95

THE BLUE AND THE GRAY: America's Civil War 1861-1865   by Carol Hauswald and Earl Bitoy (1992)
          ZP20-W . . . $19.95

THE RENAISSANCE: 1300-1600 A.D. Man, the Measure of All Things
by Jennifer Moreland (1988)   ZP08-W . . . $19.95

THE INDUSTRIAL REVOLUTION OF THE NINETEENTH CENTURY:
by Jennifer Moreland (1990)   ZP18-W . . . $19.95

EARLY JAPAN
by Ruth Patzman (1983)   ZP05-W . . . $19.95

ANCIENT CIVILIZATIONS
by Clements, Domin, Tanner (1983)   ZP02-W . . . $19.95

MIDDLE AGES
by Joey Tanner (1981)   ZP07-W . . . $19.95

THE JADE GARDEN: Ancient to Modern China
by Carol Hauswald (1991)   ZP19-W . . . $19.95

ANCIENT GREECE AND ROME
by Clements, Domin, Tanner (1983)   ZP04-W . . . $19.95

WASSILY KANDINSKY
by Stephany Grassinger (1980)   ZM05-W . . . $19.95

OLD RUSSIA: 1400–1917
by Diane Jones (1989)   ZP17-W . . . $19.95

THE AMERICAS
by Gael Beaham (1983)   ZP01-W . . . $19.95

ANCIENT EGYPT
by Clements, Domin, Tanner (1983)   ZP03-W . . . $19.95

COLUMBUS ENCOUNTER
by Rosemary Tweet and Marsie Habib (1992)
          ZP22-W . . . $19.95

EARLY PEOPLE
by Beaham and Tanner (1983)   ZP06-W . . . $19.95

You can also request a free copy of our current catalog showing other learning materials that foster whole-brain learning, creative thinking, and self-awareness.